The best recipes

TABLE OF CONTENTS

OLIVE LOVER'S CHEESE BALL

30 minutes

5-8 servings

INGREDIENTS

8 oz.	cream cheese, softened	250 g
1	large garlic clove, crushed	1
1/2 cup	finely chopped celery	125 mL
1/2 cup	chopped green onions	125 mL
1/2 cup	finely chopped green pepper	125 mL
1/2 cup	chopped, stuffed green olives	125 mL
2 cups	grated cheddar cheese	500 mL

INSTRUCTIONS

1. Mix all together.
2. Form into a ball or place in a bowl.
3. Serve with crackers.

BLUE CHEESE COUNTRY BUNS

10 minutes

20 minutes

8-12 servings

INGREDIENTS

8 oz.	wedge blue cheese (approx. 1 cup [250mL])	250 g
1/2 cup	melted butter	125 mL
12 oz.	pkg. refrigerator buns (10 buns)	340 g

INSTRUCTIONS

1. Grease or spray a 10" (25 cm) round casserole or a 9" (23 cm) square baking dish.

2. Crumble the blue cheese over the bottom of the dish. Pour the butter evenly over the cheese.

3. Cut each bun in quarters and layer them evenly over the cheese. Bake in a preheated 350° F (180° C) oven for 20 minutes (they will rise in the oven). Serve immediately.

BLUE CHEESE COUNTRY BUNS

FISH BALLS

30 minutes

3-4 minutes

4 dozen

INGREDIENTS

	vegetable oil for deep-frying	
1 cup	flaked cooked fish	250 mL
1 cup	mashed potatoes	250 mL
2	eggs	2
1/2 cup	fine cracker crumbs	125 mL
2 tbsp.	DLS*	30 mL
1 tsp.	dried dillweed	5 mL
1/4 cup	parmesan cheese	60 mL
1/2 cup	fine cracker crumbs	125 mL

INSTRUCTIONS

1. Heat the vegetable oil in a deep-fryer or heavy pot to 375° F (190° C). It should be at a depth of about 3" (7 cm) in the heavy pot or follow the manufacturer's recommendation for the deep fryer.

2. Mix the next 7 ingredients together well. Form into 1" (2.5 cm) balls and roll in the second measurement of cracker crumbs, to coat the fish balls.

3. Drop the fish balls carefully into the hot oil and fry until a golden brown. This takes only 3–4 minutes. Drain and serve.

SERVING SUGGESTIONS

We like to put a small bowl of sauce in the middle of a platter and surround it with fish balls. Looks great and tastes great!

*For Dymond Lake Seasoning substitute 1 tsp. (5 mL) seasoned pepper, 1/2 tsp. (2 mL) salt, 1/4 tsp. (1 mL) oregano, 1 tsp. (5 mL) celery flakes, 1 tbsp. (15 mL) parsley flakes.

FISH BALLS

CARIBOU BACON WRAPS

marinate 8-12 hours

20 minutes

20 minutes

serving size varies

INGREDIENTS

Wraps:

1-1 1/2 lb.	caribou meat (or moose, goose, duck or beef), cut into bite-sized cubes	450 - 680 g
8 oz.	cream cheese block (not spreadable)	250 g
	pickled jalapenos, sliced	
2 lb.	bacon slices, cut in half (or thirds, if you are using thick bacon)	908 g
	round toothpicks for assembly	

Meat marinade (optional, we suggest if using moose):
  ranch dressing

INSTRUCTIONS

1. The day before assembling your wraps, use ranch dressing to marinate your meat, just enough to coat it. Place the meat in a plastic or glass container, cover and marinate overnight. If you have a favourite meat marinade you should feel free to experiment.

2. When you're ready to assemble your wraps, lay out all your ingredients as follows: (L to R) bacon, cubed meat, cream cheese, jalapeño slices, toothpicks.

3. Take a half slice of bacon, place a cube of meat at one end, top with a teaspoon of cream cheese, add a slice of jalapeño, roll tightly and spear with a toothpick.

4. Repeat Step 3 until all wraps are assembled.

5. Wraps can be cooked fresh or frozen for future use. If freezing, place in rows on a cookie sheet, put cookie sheet in the freezer until wraps are frozen and then transfer to freezer bags or containers.

CARIBOU BACON WRAPS (CONTINUED)

6. When you're ready to cook your wraps, preheat BBQ to extra hot. If cooking from frozen, BBQ on high for approximately 20 minutes. If cooking from fresh, BBQ on high for 12 minutes. Wraps are done when bacon is a bit crispy, but the caribou is still pink inside.

CARIBOU BACON WRAPS

BAKED BRIE WITH CRANBERRY CHUTNEY

10 minutes

15-20 minutes

20 servings

INGREDIENTS

Ginger Cranberry Chutney:

1 cup	fresh or frozen cranberries	250 mL
2/3 cup	sugar	150 mL
1/3 cup	cider vinegar	75 mL
2 tbsp.	water	30 mL
2 tsp.	grated fresh ginger	10 mL
1/4 tsp.	cinnamon	1 mL
1/8 tsp.	cloves	0.5 mL
2 lb.	round of brie cheese	1 kg
	crackers or sliced baguette	

INSTRUCTIONS

1. Combine the chutney ingredients in a saucepan. Bring to a boil; reduce heat and simmer over low heat until thickened, about 15 minutes.
2. Place the Brie in a baking dish that fits, with just a little room left over. Score the top of the cheese into diamond shapes.
3. Spoon the chutney over the cheese.
4. Bake at 350° F (180° C) for 15-20 minutes or microwave for about 2 – 3 minutes, or until cheese is soft. Serve with crackers or a sliced baguette.

NOTE

The chutney may be refrigerated for up to a week, or frozen for longer storage. It may also be served with meat.

VARIATION

There is enough chutney to accommodate 4, 4 1/2 oz. (125 g) rounds of Brie if you prefer.

BAKED BRIE WITH CRANBERRY CHUTNEY

JEANNE'S MAGIC DISAPPEARING CHICKEN WINGS

10 minutes

1 1/2 hours

18–20 servings**

INGREDIENTS

3 lb.	chicken wings	1.5 kg
1 cup	flour	250 mL
1 tsp.	DLS* or 1/2 tsp. (2 mL) salt and 1/2 tsp. (2 mL) pepper	5 mL
3	eggs, beaten	3

Tangy Sauce:

3 tbsp.	soy sauce	45 mL
3 tbsp.	water	45 mL
3/4 cup	white sugar	175 mL
1/2 cup	vinegar	125 mL
1/2 tsp.	salt	2 mL

INSTRUCTIONS

1. Cut off wing tips and discard or freeze for another use. Cut remaining wings in two pieces. (You will now have one piece that looks like a tiny drumstick and one piece that still looks like a wing – sort of.)

2. Mix flour with DLS* in a small, shallow pan. Dip wings in beaten egg, then roll in the flour mixture.

3. Place wings on a well-oiled baking sheet and bake at 400° F (200° C) for 1/2 hour, or until well browned.

4. Remove the wings to a casserole or roaster. Combine all sauce ingredients and pour evenly over wings. Bake, UNCOVERED, at 350° F (180° C) for one hour. Stir once during baking.

NOTE

These are best when the sauce thickens and becomes sticky. Make lots! These wings do a disappearing act!

*See page 8 for a note on how to substitute for DLS (Dymond Lake Seasoning)

**Serves 18–20 as a taste teaser or 8 for dinner.

SPINACH AND MUSHROOM MELTS

5 minutes   5 minutes   8-10 servings

INGREDIENTS

1/2 cup	butter	125 mL
5	garlic cloves	5
3 cups	sliced mushrooms	750 mL
	DLS* or salt and pepper to taste	
10 oz.	fresh baby spinach	300 g
1/2 loaf	French bread, toasted	1/2 loaf
	mozzarella or your favourite cheese, sliced	
	sliced sun-dried tomatoes in oil (optional)	

INSTRUCTIONS

1. In a frying pan, melt the butter and sauté the garlic and mushrooms until the mushrooms are golden brown, about five minutes. Add DLS* and spinach. Stir until the spinach is just wilted, about 1–2 minutes.

2. Heap the spinach mixture on toasted French bread. Top with cheese and broil until the cheese melts. Garnish with tomatoes if desired.

*See page 8 for a note on how to substitute for DLS (Dymond Lake Seasoning)

GOOSE TIDBITS

10 minutes

10 minutes

serving size varies

INGREDIENTS

3-4	goose breasts	
2 tbsp.	butter	30 mL
1/4 cup	white vermouth	60 mL
	DLS* or seasoned pepper to taste	

INSTRUCTIONS

1. Lay the goose breast flat on the cutting board and, with a sharp knife, slice horizontally to make very thin slices.

2. Melt the butter in a heavy frying pan over medium-high heat until it is sizzling.

3. Lay the goose slices in the frying pan and sprinkle liberally with DLS* or seasoned pepper. They should brown quite quickly. If they do not, turn up the heat a bit. When they are nicely browned on one side turn them over, sprinkle liberally again with DLS* or seasoned pepper. Brown for about a minute.

4. Add in the vermouth and let the breasts simmer for about a minute.

5. Remove from pan and serve immediately, with toothpicks.

*See page 8 for a note on how to substitute for DLS (Dymond Lake Seasoning)

SOUSED SALMON OR TROUT BARBECUE

marinate for 4 - 6 hours

7 minutes

6-8 servings

INGREDIENTS

Rye, Garlic and Soy Marinade:

3/4 cup	soy sauce	175 mL
1 1/4 cups	vegetable oil	300 mL
1	garlic clove, crushed	1
1/4 cup	rye whisky	60 mL
2 tbsp.	sugar (optional)	30 mL
2	large salmon or lake trout fillets with skin	2
	pepper	

INSTRUCTIONS

1. Combine all of the marinade ingredients in a shallow non-aluminum container.

2. Lay the cleaned fish in the marinade. Sprinkle with pepper. Marinate for 4–6 hours, turning once.

3. Preheat the barbeque to high. Lay the fillets, skin-side down, directly on the hot grill. Close the lid and barbeque for seven minutes. There will be lots of smoke, and the skin will burn, but the fish will be moist and delicious. Serve as a meal or as an appetizer.

SOUSED SALMON OR TROUT BARBECUE

VEGGIE STRUDELS

30 minutes

2 hours

makes 2 dozen

INGREDIENTS

1 tbsp.	olive oil	15 mL
1 tbsp.	butter	15 mL
1 1/2 cups	finely chopped, mixed green, red, yellow peppers	375 mL
1/2 cup	diced onions	125 mL
1 1/2 tbsp.	finely diced garlic	22 mL
1/4 cup	finely diced celery	60 mL
1/4 cup	finely diced carrots	60 mL
1 1/2 tsp.	DLS*	7 mL
1 tsp.	fresh, coarsely ground black pepper	5 mL
1 tbsp.	shredded fresh basil or 1 tsp. (5 mL) dried	15 mL
1/2 cup	finely chopped zucchini	125 mL
1/2 cup	finely chopped sliced mushrooms	125 mL
1 1/2 cups	crumbled feta cheese	375 mL
18 sheets	phyllo pastry	18 sheets
	melted butter	

INSTRUCTIONS

1. Heat the olive oil and butter in a large frying pan. Add the peppers, onions, garlic, celery, carrots, DLS*, black pepper and basil. Sauté the vegetables over medium-low heat, to make them sweat, about 10 minutes. Add mushrooms and zucchini halfway through. Pour everything into a fine strainer to drain off excess liquid. Allow to cool.

2. When the mixture is cooled, stir in the feta and prepare to wrap.

3. Cut each sheet of phyllo into 4, 4 x 12" (10 x 30 cm) strips.

4. Using 3 strips per strudel, brush each strip with melted butter, placing them on top of the other. Place a healthy amount of veggie mix on one end of the strip and fold it into triangles, keeping the corners as tight as possible.

5. Place triangle strudels on greased baking sheets. Brush the tops with melted butter. Bake at 400° F (200° C) for 15–20 minutes. Remove to a rack to cool slightly. Serve warm.

NOTE

These freeze well. *See page 8 for a note on how to substitute for DLS (Dymond Lake Seasoning)

CURRIED SQUASH SOUP

20 minutes

30 minutes

4 servings

INGREDIENTS

6 cups	peeled, chunked butternut squash	1.5 L
3/4 cup	chopped onion	175 mL
2 tbsp.	chopped fresh cilantro	30 mL
1	garlic clove, crushed	1
2 cups	chicken stock	500 mL
1/2 tsp.	salt	2 mL
1 tbsp.	fresh lemon juice	15 mL
1/2 tsp.	cumin	2 mL
1/2 tsp.	curry powder	2 mL
1/2 tsp.	pepper	2 mL
1/2 cup	cream	125 mL

INSTRUCTIONS

1. In a large saucepan, bring all of the ingredients, except the cream, to a boil. Simmer until the vegetables are very tender, about 30 minutes. Remove from the heat and puree until smooth.

2. Add the cream and reheat, but do not boil. Taste and adjust seasonings.

HAMBURGER SOUP

30 minutes

2 hours

10 servings

INGREDIENTS

1 1/2 lb.	ground beef	750 g
1	medium onion, chopped	1
28 oz.	can diced tomatoes	796 mL
6 cups	beef broth	1.5 L
4	carrots, chopped	4
4	celery ribs, chopped	4
1/2	green pepper, chopped	1/2
1/2 cup	pot barley	125 mL
2 tbsp.	parsley	30 mL
1 tbsp.	DLS*	15 mL

INSTRUCTIONS

1. Brown meat and onions. Drain well.

2. Combine all ingredients in a large pot. Bring to a boil. Simmer, covered, for at least 2 hours to make sure the barley is cooked.

3. Taste to adjust seasonings.

NOTES

Makes at least 10 servings and freezes well.

*See page 8 for a note on how to substitute for DLS (Dymond Lake Seasoning)

HAMBURGER SOUP

SIMPLY DELICIOUS MUSHROOM SOUP

15 minutes

20 minutes

4 servings

INGREDIENTS

1/4 cup	butter	60 mL
1/2 cup	chopped onion, in 1/2" (1.3 cm) chunks	125 mL
1/4 cup	chopped celery	60 mL
1	large garlic clove, chopped	1
2 tsp.	DLS*	10 mL
1/2 tsp.	salt	2 mL
2 cups	sliced button mushrooms	500 mL
1 cup	sliced portabella or shitake mushrooms, in 1/2" (1.3 cm) pieces	125 mL
3 tbsp.	flour	45 mL
2 cups	half-and-half cream or evaporated milk	500 mL
2 cups	milk	500 mL

INSTRUCTIONS

1. Melt the butter in a medium-sized saucepan. Add the onions, stirring to coat with butter. Turn the heat to low; cover and cook the onions for five minutes, stirring twice.

2. Add celery and garlic and cook over medium heat for 2–3 minutes. Add DLS*, salt and mushrooms. Continue to cook, stirring occasionally until the mushrooms are cooked, about five minutes.

3. Add 1 tbsp. (15 mL) of butter and cook until melted. Remove the saucepan from the heat. Stir in the flour until it is absorbed by the butter. Slowly add half-and-half, stirring constantly to keep the mixture smooth. Cook over medium heat until it simmers. Simmer for 2–3 minutes, stirring constantly. Stir in the milk and heat just until the soup comes to a boil.

NOTES

*See page 8 for a note on how to substitute for DLS (Dymond Lake Seasoning)

SIMPLY DELICIOUS MUSHROOM SOUP

BROCCOLI SALAD

30 minutes

6-10 servings

INGREDIENTS

3	large broccoli stems with florets	3
1 lb.	bacon, fried crisp and crumbled	500 g
1/2 cup	raisins	125 mL
1/2 cup	sliced almonds or sunflower seeds	125 mL
1	small red onion, halved, thinly sliced	1

Creamy Cider Dressing:

1 cup	mayonnaise or similar salad dressing	250 mL
1/4 cup	sugar	60 mL
2 tbsp.	cider vinegar	30 mL

INSTRUCTIONS

1. Peel broccoli stems and cut into bite-sized pieces. Cut up the florets and add to the stems with the bacon, raisins, almonds and red onion.

2. Mix the dressing ingredients together with a whisk.

3. Add the dressing to the broccoli mixture. This keeps well for 1 day.

SERVING SUGGESTION

This is great on a buffet table, but don't limit its potential. It is great with chicken, fish, beef, pork or whatever.

BROCCOLI SALAD

GREEK SALAD

marinate times varies

20 minutes

6-8 servings

INGREDIENTS

1/2	red onion, halved and sliced thinly	1/2
4	large tomatoes, halved and sliced	4
1	English cucumber, halved lengthwise, and sliced	1
1	green pepper, halved and sliced	1
8	leaves romaine lettuce, torn	8
1 cup	pitted black olives, whole or sliced	250 mL
3/4 cup	crumbled feta cheese	175 mL

Greek Dressing:

1 cup	olive oil	250 mL
1/2 cup	red wine vinegar	125 mL
1 tsp.	salt	5 mL
1/4 tsp.	pepper	1 mL
1 tsp.	dried oregano	5 mL
1 tsp.	dried basil	5 mL
2	small garlic cloves, crushed	2

INSTRUCTIONS

1. Prepare the dressing first. Shake all the dressing ingredients in a jar or mix with a hand blender.

2. Marinate the sliced red onion in about 1/2 cup (125 mL) of the dressing while you are preparing the rest of the salad. The longer you let the onions marinate, the milder they will taste.

3. Place the remaining ingredients in a large mixing bowl.

4. Just before serving, add the 1/2 cup (125 mL) of dressing and the onions to the salad. Toss and add extra dressing if desired. Add only enough dressing to lightly coat the salad ingredients. The rest will keep in a glass jar in the refrigerator for weeks.

ONION SALAD

marinate 12 hours

10 minutes

16-20 servings

INGREDIENTS

6	Spanish onions*, very thinly sliced	6
1/2 cup	vinegar	125 mL
1/2 cup	water	125 mL
3/4 cup	sugar	175 mL
2 tsp.	salt	10 mL
1 1/4 cup	mayonnaise or similar salad dressing	300 mL
2 tbsp.	celery seed	30 mL

INSTRUCTIONS

1. Slice the onions very thinly and place them in a plastic or glass dish.

2. Combine the vinegar, water, sugar and salt. Mix well to dissolve the sugar and salt. Pour over the onions and mix well. Put a plate on top of the onions and set a weight on it. A plastic bottle of oil or vinegar works well. Let the onions sit on the counter all day – overnight is best.

3. Drain the onions. (You will wonder where all the liquid came from!)

4. Combine the dressing and celery seed and toss with the onions. Put into a serving bowl and serve.

SERVING SUGGESTION

This is great served with beef or Jalapeño Goose. If there is any left over, pile it on a bun with beef or goose the next day for a super lunch!

NOTE

*We often don't have Spanish onions, so will use whatever is at hand. Strong onions can be toned down quickly by pouring hot water over the slices (especially if they have been separated into rings), allowed to sit for a while (five minutes will do) and drained – before continuing with the marinade.

MINTY BEET SALAD

| 30 minutes | 3-5 minutes | 8-10 servings |

The sweet crunch of apples with the tart tang of beets awakens the taste buds! If you take this salad to a potluck, be prepared to share the recipe. Our thanks to Brian, who brought this to a potluck and shared it with us.

INGREDIENTS

3 cups	coarsely chopped pickled beets	750 mL
2 cups	coarsely chopped apple	500 mL
1 1/2 cups	coarsely chopped green onions	375 mL
3/4 cup	coarsely chopped celery stalks	175 mL
2 tbsp.	coarsely chopped mint leaves (optional)	30 mL

Mint Dressing:

1/2 cup	chopped fresh mint leaves or 1 tbsp. (15mL) dried	125 mL
1 cup	pickled beet brine, drained from the pickled beets	250 mL
2 tbsp.	sugar	30 mL
2 tsp.	white wine vinegar	10 mL
1/8 tsp.	dried tarragon	0.8 mL

INSTRUCTIONS

1. Combine all of the dressing ingredients in a saucepan and bring to a boil. Let simmer for 3–5 minutes, stirring occasionally.

2. Remove from the heat and strain into a bowl.

3. Place the beets, apple, onion, celery and mint in a large bowl. Pour about half the dressing over the salad and toss unitl well mixed. Add more dressing as needed to coat the ingredients. Taste for seasoning and add salt and pepper as needed.

4. Chill the salad before serving.

EGYPTIAN SALAD

20 minutes

6 servings

INGREDIENTS

8 cups	torn romaine lettuce	2 L
1/2 cup	crumbled feta cheese	125 mL
1 cup	seedless grapes, red and/or green	250 mL
1/4 cup	thinly sliced red or sweet onions (optional)	60 mL

Lemon Dressing:

1/4 cup	olive oil	60 mL
2 tbsp.	lemon juice	30 mL
1 tsp.	sugar	5 mL
	pepper (optional)	

INSTRUCTIONS

1. Prepare salad ingredients and combine in a large bowl.

2. Mix dressing ingredients and toss with salad ingredients just before serving.

EXOTIC SPINACH SALAD

30 minutes

6 servings

We've never served this without having to give the recipe away afterwards.

INGREDIENTS

8 cups	torn spinach	2 L
1	mango, sliced	1
1	kiwi, sliced	1
1 cup	strawberries, sliced	250 mL

Sesame and Poppy Seed Dressing:

1/3 cup	sugar	75 mL
2 tbsp.	sesame seeds	30 mL
1 tbsp.	poppy seeds	15 mL
1/2 tsp.	grated onion	2 mL
1/4 tsp.	Worcestershire sauce	1 mL
1/4 tsp.	paprika	1 mL
1/2 cup	vegetable oil	125 mL
1/4 cup	raspberry or cider vinegar	60 mL

INSTRUCTIONS

1. Prepare spinach and fruit and place in a salad bowl.
2. Combine all dressing ingredients, except vinegar, in blender. Slowly add vinegar and blend until dressing thickens.
3. Just before serving, toss salad with desired amount of dressing.

VARIATIONS

Use nectarines if mangoes aren't available. Also try raspberries.

MARIE'S WILD RICE CASSEROLE SUPREME

90 minutes

30 minutes

6 servings

INGREDIENTS

1 cup	uncooked whole kernel wild rice	250 mL
3 cups	beef broth	750 mL
1/4 tsp.	thyme	1 mL
1/4 tsp.	basil	1 mL
1/2 cup	butter or margarine	125 mL
1/3 cup	finely chopped onions	75 mL
1/2 lb.	fresh mushroom, sliced or 10 oz. (284 mL) can	250 g
1/2 cup	evaporated milk or light cream	125 mL

INSTRUCTIONS

1. Rinse wild rice with cold water and place in a large pot with the beef broth, thyme and basil. Bring to a boil, cover and simmer for one hour, or until tender. Remove from the heat and let sit for 30 minutes to absorb the remaining liquid.

2. Melt the butter in a large frying pan. Add the onions, and sauté until translucent. Add the mushrooms and brown lightly.

3. Combine the rice, mushroom, onion mixture and evaporated milk. Place in a greased 1 1/2-quart (1.5 L) casserole dish.

4. Bake in a 350°F (180°C) oven for 30 minutes, until heated through.

TIME-SAVING TIP

You can make this a day or two ahead and refrigerate it. Just increase the oven time by 15 minutes. It even freezes well, so double the recipe and freeze a batch for another day.

COOKING TIP

Cooking time for wild rice varies according to how the rice has been parched (dried).

MARIE'S WILD RICE CASSEROLE SUPREME

MOZZARELLA MASHED POTATOES

30 minutes

1 hour

6-8 servings

INGREDIENTS

3 lb.	potatoes, peeled and quartered	1.5 kg
8 slices	bacon, diced	8
2	garlic cloves, crushed	2
1 cup	sour cream	250 mL
1/4 cup	butter, room temperature	60 mL
1 tsp.	salt	5 mL
1/2 tsp.	pepper	2 mL
1/4 cup	chopped chives	60 mL
1 cup	grated mozzarella cheese	250 mL

INSTRUCTIONS

1. In a large saucepan, cook potatoes in boiling salted water until tender.

2. While the potatoes are cooking, fry the diced bacon until crisp. Remove the bacon from the pan, drain off all but about 1 tbsp. (15 mL) of drippings and add garlic. Sauté over medium-low heat for two minutes. Remove from the pan and add to the bacon.

3. When the potatoes are tender, drain well. Mash with a potato masher until smooth. Add the bacon, garlic, sour cream, butter, salt, pepper, chives and the cheese, mixing well.

4. Turn the potato mixture into a greased 1 1/2 - 2-quart (1.5–2 L) casserole dish. Bake, covered, at 350°F (180°C) for 45 minutes, removing the cover for the last 15 minutes of baking time.

NOTE

If you make these ahead, allow them to cool, then cover and refrigerate or freeze. Let them thaw completely in the refrigerator overnight, before baking, If you forget to do this, add up to 30 minutes to the baking time.

MARIE'S MOM'S YORKSHIRE PUDDING

1-4 hours

15 minutes

12 servings

We included this recipe because it is such a hard one to find and it is so good.

INGREDIENTS

4	eggs	4
1 cup	flour	250 mL
1 cup	milk	250 mL
1/2 tsp.	salt	2 mL
	oil	

INSTRUCTIONS

1. Beat eggs, flour, milk and salt well with a wire whisk or hand beater. Let the batter sit on the counter for 1–4 hours – it must be at room temperature. Beat the batter again, just before using.

2. About 20 minutes before serving, put 1 tsp. (5 mL) oil in each of 12 muffin cups and heat in 450°F (230°C) oven until oil is hot, about two minutes.

3. Remove the pan from the oven and divide the batter between the cups. Cups will be about half full. Return the pan to the oven and bake for 15 minutes.

4. Turn Yorkshires out of muffin cups and serve immediately.

COOKING TIP

Yorkshires will rise high and be well browned when done. BUT they will sink when removed from oven. This is normal!

My mom also used to make this in a round, Pyrex casserole dish. To serve, she cut it in wedges, like a pie. That method makes a much denser and heavier Yorkshire but I'm sure that's how it was done originally.

SWEET AND SOUR BAKED BEANS

30 minutes

1 hour

10-12 servings

INGREDIENTS

19 oz.	can garbanzo beans* (chickpeas), drained	540 mL
14 oz.	EACH can red kidney and lima beans*, drained	398 mL
28 oz.	can Boston baked beans	796 mL
8	bacon slices	8
2	large onions, sliced or chopped	2
1	garlic clove, crushed	1
1 cup	brown sugar	250 mL
1 tsp.	dry mustard	5 mL
1 tsp.	salt	5 mL
1/2 cup	vinegar	125 mL

INSTRUCTIONS

1. Combine the beans in a 4-quart (4 L) ovenproof casserole or pan. (Don't forget to drain all but the Boston beans.)

2. Fry the bacon until crisp. Crumble bacon into the beans. Reserve 2 tbsp. (30 mL) bacon fat in the pan and discard the rest.

3. Sauté the onions and garlic in the bacon fat over medium heat until onions are translucent. Add brown sugar, mustard, salt and vinegar. Heat to boiling. Add to the beans in the casserole.

4. Bake at 350°F (180°C) for 1 hour, or until bubbly.

*Any similar beans may be substituted except for the Boston baked beans.

BÉCHAMEL TURNIP

30 minutes

30 minutes

8 servings

INGREDIENTS

2 cups	cooked, mashed turnip	500 mL
1	egg	1
2 tbsp.	butter	30 mL
1 1/4 tsp.	savory	6 mL
1/2 tsp.	salt	2 mL
1/4 tsp.	pepper	1 mL

Béchamel Sauce:

1 cup	milk	250 mL
1	small onion, peeled and quartered	1
5	whole cloves	5
4	peppercorns	4
1	small carrot, chopped	1
1	bay leaf	1
2	sprigs of parsley	2
3 tbsp.	butter	45 mL
3 tbsp.	flour	45 mL
1/2 cup	grated cheese for topping	125 mL

INSTRUCTIONS

1. Mash the hot, cooked turnip with the egg, butter, savory, salt and pepper.

2. To make the Béchamel Sauce, in a small saucepan, bring the milk, onion, cloves, peppercorns, carrot, bay leaf and parsley to a boil. Remove from heat; cover and let sit for 15 minutes. Strain out all the solids.

3. In a small saucepan, melt the butter over medium-low heat. Stir in the flour and heat for one minute. Gradually whisk in a cup (250 mL) of the strained milk, whisking to keep it smooth. Bring to a boil, reduce heat and simmer gently for about five minutes, to cook the flour.

4. Pour sauce over turnip. Sprinkle cheese over sauce. Bake uncovered, at 350°F (180°C) for 30 minutes, or until bubbly and heated through.

JALAPEÑO GOOSE BREASTS SUPREME

marinate 1-2 hours

10 minutes

15 minutes

serving size varies

INGREDIENTS

young goose breasts
soy sauce
fresh garlic cloves, crushed
pickled jalapeño peppers and juice
bacon drippings

INSTRUCTIONS

1. Use approximately three breasts per person. Put a single layer of goose breasts in a glass or plastic dish (a plastic ice-cream pail works well).

2. Spread with two crushed garlic cloves and pour over 1/4 cup (60 mL) soy sauce.

3. Add another layer of breasts, crushed garlic and soy sauce until all breasts have been used. Be sure that the soy sauce almost covers the meat.

4. About an hour before serving, remove the breasts from the marinade and put a small slit on each side of the breast with a sharp knife. Into each of these slits stuff a small slice of pickled jalapeño pepper.

5. Now pile the breasts back into the dish or onto a tray to be taken out to the barbecue. On the tray put a small dish of melted bacon drippings and a dish of jalapeño juice from the pickle jar. You will also need a pair of tongs, a pastry brush and a small knife to check for doneness.

6. Barbecue the breasts over medium-high heat, brushing with bacon drippings and jalapeño juice until medium (still pink in the middle), about 4–6 minutes per side. Do not overcook.

SERVING SUGGESTION

We serve this with Marie's Wild Rice Casserole, Onion Salad, Broccoli Salad, fresh rolls (of course) and any one of our great desserts.

JALAPEÑO GOOSE BREASTS SUPREME

— mains —

ALMOND-CRUSTED TROUT WITH LEEK AND LEMON CREAM

30 minutes

30 minutes

6 servings

INGREDIENTS

Leek and Lemon Cream Sauce:

2	medium leeks or 2 cups (500 mL) finely chopped onion**	2
2 tbsp.	butter	30 mL
3 tbsp.	fresh lemon juice	45 mL
1 cup	whipping cream	250 mL
	salt and pepper to taste	

Almond-Crusted Trout:

1 cup	chopped sliced almonds	250 mL
1 tbsp.	chopped fresh parsley or 1 tsp. (5 mL) dried	15 mL
1 tbsp.	grated lemon peel	15 mL
1/2 tsp.	salt	2 mL
1/8 tsp.	ground black pepper	0.8 mL
1/2 cup	flour	125 mL
6 x 6 oz.	skinless trout fillets	6 x 170 g
	DLS* or salt and pepper	
1	large egg, beaten	1
2 tbsp.	butter	30 mL
2 tbsp.	olive oil	30 mL

INSTRUCTIONS

TO MAKE THE SAUCE

1. Wash leeks thoroughly. Cut in half and slice thinly (use only the white and pale green parts). In a heavy saucepan, sauté leeks in butter for two minutes over medium-high heat. Reduce heat, cover and cook until tender, about 20 minutes.

2. Reduce heat to medium. Add lemon juice and stir until the liquid evaporates, about one minute. Stir in cream. Simmer until slightly reduced, about two minutes. Cool slightly.

3. Season to taste with salt and pepper. If not using immediately, refrigerate until ready to serve; then reheat.

TO PREPARE THE TROUT

1. Combine the almonds, parsley, lemon peel, salt and pepper on a plate. Place the flour on another plate.

2. Sprinkle trout with DLS*. Dredge the trout with flour, shaking off excess. Lightly brush one side of each trout fillet with beaten egg. Press brushed side of fillets into almond mixture, pressing lightly to make it adhere. Set fillets aside until all are prepared.

3. Melt 1 tbsp. (15 mL) butter and 1 tbsp. (15mL) oil in a heavy, large skillet over medium heat. Add fillets, almond side down. Cook in two batches if necessary. Cook until the almond crust is brown, about five minutes. Turn fillets over and sauté until cooked through, about 3–5 minutes. Serve with the reserved sauce.

NOTE

*See page 8 for a note on how to substitute for DLS (Dymond Lake Seasoning)

**Pour boiling water over onions – let sit for 5 minutes, drain and use as above.

ALMOND-CRUSTED TROUT WITH LEEK AND LEMON CREAM

CRUSTED CARIBOU TENDERLOIN WITH MUSHROOM AND RED WINE REDUCTION

| marinate up to 24 hours | 1 hour | 20-25 minutes | 8 servings |

Two thumbs up is what the guests we invited to our testing gave this dish. Use any tenderloin available, moose, elk, deer, beef or pork – but DO plan ahead, and DON'T let the long name put you off. This is definitely a company pleaser!

INGREDIENTS

1 tbsp.	coriander or mustard seeds	15 mL
1 tbsp.	black peppercorns	15 mL
3 tbsp.	dijon mustard	45 mL
2 tbsp.	minced fresh thyme leaves or 1 tbsp. (15 mL) dried	30 mL
3 lb.	caribou tenderloin or back strip	1.5 kg
2 cups	soft white bread crumbs	500 mL
1/2 cup	finely chopped fresh parsley or 2 tbsp. (30mL) dried	125 mL
2–3 tbsp.	olive oil	30-45 mL
1 tsp.	salt	5 mL

Mushroom and Red Wine Reduction:

1 cup	chopped shiitake or portabella or white button mushrooms	250 mL
2	garlic cloves, minced or chopped	2
1/2 cup	onion, finely chopped	125 mL
1 tbsp.	olive oil	15 mL
2 cups	dry red wine (Merlot or Beaujolais)	500 mL
2 cups	beef broth	500 mL
1 tbsp.	minced, fresh thyme leaves or 1 tsp. (5 mL) dried	15 mL
1 tbsp.	sugar	15 mL
2 tsp.	DLS* or 1/2 tsp. (2 mL) salt and 1/2 tsp. (2 mL) pepper	10 mL
1/4 cup	soft butter	60 mL

INSTRUCTIONS

1. Crush the coriander seeds and black peppercorns. Add to the mustard and thyme leaves in a small bowl. Mix well.

2. Pat tenderloin dry and place it on a sheet of plastic wrap. Coat it completely with the mustard mixture. Roll the plastic wrap around the tenderloin and place in a plastic bag in the refrigerator for up to 24 hours.

3. Stir together the bread crumbs and parsley. Stir in 2 tbsp. (30 mL) of olive oil to moisten. Add a bit more olive oil if it seems too dry. Completely coat caribou with crumb mixture, pressing it into the meat. Let sit, uncovered, at room temperature, for at least an hour before roasting.

4. To make the reduction, sauté mushrooms, garlic and onion in olive oil for 5–8 minutes, or until onions are softened. Add remaining ingredients, except butter. Bring to a boil and simmer until liquid has reduced to 2 cups (500 mL), about 30 minutes. Stir in the butter. Keep warm until ready to serve.

5. Preheat oven to 450°F (230°C). Sprinkle the tenderloin evenly on all sides with salt, patting the salt into the bread crumbs. Place on an oiled rack over a shallow roasting pan. Roast for 20–25 minutes, until done to your likeness: 140°F (60°C) for rare; 150°F (65°C) for medium-rare. Let the tenderloin sit, loosely covered with foil, for 10 minutes before carving. Cut into 1 1/2" (4 cm) slices and arrange on a platter.

6. Either spoon the Mushroom and Red Wine Reduction over the sliced tenderloin or pass the reduction in a gravy boat.

NOTE

The cooking time may vary with the size of the tenderloin.

*See page 8 for a note on how to substitute for DLS (Dymond Lake Seasoning)

CRUSTED CARIBOU TENDERLOIN WITH MUSHROOM AND RED WINE REDUCTION

PRIME RIB WITH MUSHROOM AU JUS

10 minutes

20-30 minutes per pound

10-12 servings

INGREDIENTS

8 -10 lb.	prime rib roast	3.5 – 4.5 kg
	DLS*	
3	garlic cloves , crushed	3

Mushroom Au Jus:

1 1/2 oz.	pkg. onion soup mix	40 g
10 oz.	can beef consommé	284 mL
10 oz.	can sliced mushrooms, undrained	284 mL
2 cups	water	500 mL

INSTRUCTIONS

TO PREPARE THE ROAST

1. Bring roast to room temperature before proceeding and preheat the oven to 425°F (220°C).
2. Place the roast, fat side up, in a large heavy roasting pan. Rub crushed garlic all over the top and sides.
3. Sprinkle the roast liberally with at least 2 tbsp. (30 mL) of DLS*. The top of the roast should be well covered.
4. Roast, UNCOVERED, for 15 minutes at 425°F (220°C). Reduce the temperature to 325°F (160°C) and continue to roast 20 minutes per pound for rare, 25 minutes per pound for medium and 30 minutes per pound for well.
5. Remove the roast from the roaster and let it rest for 10 minutes before carving. While it is resting, prepare the Mushroom Au Jus, below.

TO MAKE THE MUSHROOMS AU JUS

1. Skim the grease from the roasting pan as best you can. It doesn't hurt to leave some behind.
2. To the roaster add the onion soup mix, beef consommé, mushrooms with liquid and the water. Simmer on low while you carve the roast.

SERVING SUGGESTION

Serve in a gravy boat. Pour it over prime rib and Yorkshire pudding. It will pool on your plate and add great flavour to your potatoes and vegetables too!

*See page 8 for a note on how to substitute for DLS (Dymond Lake Seasoning)

TARRAGON MUSHROOM CHICKEN

10 minutes

1 hour

6 servings

A hint of tarragon in a thin creamy mushroom sauce – enough to serve over noodles – succulent and simple!

INGREDIENTS

12	chicken pieces with skin	12
	butter, melted	
	DLS* or salt and seasoned pepper	
3 tbsp.	butter or margarine	45 mL
4 cups	sliced, fresh mushrooms or 2 x 10 oz. (2 x 284 mL) cans, with juice	1 L
1/4 cup	flour	60 mL
1 1/2 cups	chicken stock	375 mL
1/2 tsp.	dried tarragon or 1 tbsp. (15 mL) minced fresh	2 mL
3/4 cup	light cream or evaporated milk	175 mL
1/4 cup	white wine (optional)	60 mL
	salt and pepper to taste	

INSTRUCTIONS

1. Arrange the chicken pieces, skin side up, on a greased baking tray. Brush with melted butter and sprinkle generously with DLS*, or salt and pepper.

2. Bake at 375°F (190°C) for 30 – 40 minutes, or until skin is WELL BROWNED. Remove chicken to a 4 – 5-quart (4–5 L) casserole dish.

3. Melt butter and sauté the mushrooms. Sprinkle with the flour and stir, blending well. Gradually add the chicken broth, stirring continually to keep the sauce smooth. Add the tarragon and cook until thickened. Add cream and wine, then season to taste.

4. Pour the sauce over the chicken in the casserole dish. Bake, uncovered, at 250°F (180°C) for 30 minutes. This chicken is great served over rice or noodles.

NOTE

Increase baking time to 1 hour if you have made chicken ahead and refrigerated it.

*See page 8 for a note on how to substitute for DLS (Dymond Lake Seasoning)

CHEESE BISCUITS

20 minutes

10 - 12 minutes

makes 15 biscuits

Occasionally, you want a change from traditional tea biscuits. A hint of cheese gives a tasty alternative. These drop biscuits are ideal for the busy cook.

INGREDIENTS

2 cups	flour	500 mL
4 tsp.	baking powder	20 mL
1/2 tsp.	salt	2 mL
3/4 cup	cold butter or margarine	175 mL
2 cups	finely grated cheese*	500 mL
1 cup	water	250 mL

INSTRUCTIONS

1. Put flour, baking and salt in a bowl. Add butter and cut in with pastry blender until fairly well blended. Small lumps are all right.

2. Add cheese and stir in with fork, carefully separating any cheese that has lumped together.

3. Add water all at once and stir with a fork just until blended.

4. Drop batter by heaping tablespoons (about 25 ml) onto an ungreased baking sheet.

5. Bake at 450°F (230°C) for 10–12 minutes. Jagged peaks on the tops of the biscuits will be browned. Remove the biscuits from the tray immediately.

SERVING SUGGESTION

Serve warm for an evening snack or to accompany a light lunch.

NOTE

*Use Cheddar or mozzarella or a mixture or experiment with any hard cheese. Cheese should be only loosely packed when measuring.

RED RIVER BREAD

 2 1/2 hours

 30 minutes

 makes 5 loaves

INGREDIENTS

4 cups	lukewarm water	1 L
6 tbsp.	white sugar*	90 mL
1 tbsp.	salt*	15 mL
1/2 cup	vegetable oil	125 mL
2 cups	cooked Red River Cereal** (approximately)	500 mL
13 cups	flour (approximately)	3.25 L
2 tbsp.	instant yeast	30 mL

INSTRUCTIONS

1. In a large mixing bowl, combine water, sugar, salt, oil and cereal. If you don't have an automatic mixer, use a wire whisk and mix well.

2. Add 4 cups (1 L) of flour and the yeast. Mix well.

3. Switch to a dough hook, if you have one, and add the rest of the flour, gradually. Knead until dough isn't too sticky to handle. If kneading by hand, add as much flour as you can in the bowl, then turn out onto a FLOURED surface. Knead in the rest of the flour by hand. It may take a little MORE or a little LESS flour. Just knead the dough until it feels soft but not sticky and bounces back when pressed, 8-10 minutes.

4. Shape dough into a ball, place in a large well-greased bowl, turning dough to grease surface. Cover with a cloth. Put in a warm place and let rise until doubled in size, about an hour.

5. Punch down dough and turn out onto a GREASED surface. With a bread knife, divide dough into 5 even portions. Shape each portion into a loaf, using a kneading motion. (Or use a rolling pin to roll out dough, and then roll it into a loaf.) Whatever method you use, it might not LOOK perfect the first time, but you'll improve with practice.

6. Place loaves in well-greased 3 x 5 x 8" (7 x 13 x 20 cm) bread pans. Cover with a cloth. Let rise until the bread has risen 1" (2.5 cm) above the pans, about an hour.

7. Remove cloth and bake loaves at 350°F (180°C) for 30 minutes.

8. Remove baked loafs from oven and turn out of pans onto a cooling rack. Loaves should be brown on bottom and sides as well as on top.

NOTES

*Amounts of salt and sugar are flexible. If you want less of each, reduce salt to 2 tsp. (10 mL) and sugar to 1/4 cup (60 mL)

**If making Red River Cereal from scratch, use 1 cup (250 mL) dry cereal, boiled in 3 cups (750 mL) of water. It makes more than 2 cups (500 mL), but you can use it all in this recipe.

RED RIVER BREAD

CRUSTY ROLLS

2 hours

15 minutes

makes 18 buns

INGREDIENTS

2 cups	lukewarm water	500 mL
3 tbsp.	butter or margarine, melted	45 mL
2 tbsp.	white sugar	30 mL
2 tsp.	salt	10 mL
5 cups	flour (approximately)	1.25 mL
1	egg white	1
1 tbsp.	yeast	15 mL

Egg wash:

1	egg white	1
1 tbsp.	water	15 mL
	sesame or poppy seeds	

INSTRUCTIONS

1. Combine water, butter, salt, 1 3/4 cups (425 ml) flour, egg white and yeast in a large mixing bowl. Beat until smooth.

2. Switch to a dough hook, if you have one, and add the rest of the flour, gradually. Knead until dough isn't too sticky to handle. If kneading by hand, add as much flour as you can in the bowl, then turn out onto a FLOURED surface, and work in the rest of the flour by hand, using a kneading motion. You may need MORE or LESS flour, but knead dough until it is smooth but not sticky, and bounces back when pressed, about 8 – 10 minutes.

3. Place in a greased bowl, turning to grease top of dough. Cover and let rise in a warm place until double in bulk, about 45 minutes.

4. While you are waiting, prepare 2 cookie sheets by greasing them and sprinkling them with cornmeal.

5. Punch down dough and turn out on a greased surface. Divide dough in half. Form each half into a 9" (23 cm) roll. Cut each roll into 9 pieces. Form each piece into a smooth ball.

6. Place balls about 3" (7 cm) apart on the prepared baking sheets. Cover and let rise in a warm place until doubled in bulk, about an hour.

7. When ready to bake, brush rolls with a mixture of 1 egg white and 1 tbsp. (15 ml) water. Slit tops with a sharp knife criss-cross fashion, and sprinkle with sesame or poppy seeds.

8. Bake in hot oven, 400°F (200°C), for 15 minutes. Remove rolls from baking sheets and cool on racks.

CRANBERRY CAKE WITH BUTTER SAUCE

30 minutes

30-40 minutes

12-15 servings

This dessert is a real sleeper. To read it, it sounds "ho hum" but the first bite will pop your eyes wide open. This recipe keeps Marie and I crawling around on the tundra, making sure we have our winter supply of cranberries in the freezer. - Helen

INGREDIENTS

Cranberry Cake:

3 cups	flour	750 mL
4 tsp.	baking powder	20 mL
1/2 tsp.	salt	2 mL
3 tbsp.	butter or margarine	45 mL
1 1/2 cups	sugar	375 mL
1 1/2 tsp	vanilla	7 mL
1 1/2 cups	milk	375 mL
3 cups	cranberries	750 mL

Butter Sauce:

3/4 cup	butter or margarine	175 mL
1 1/2 cups	sugar	375 mL
3/4 cup	evaporated milk or cream	175 mL

INSTRUCTIONS

TO PREPARE THE CAKE

1. Mix the flour, baking powder and salt in a bowl and set aside.

2. Cream together the butter, sugar and vanilla. It does not get all creamy and fluffy as it does in a butter cake, as the ratio of butter to sugar is not high enough. That is the way it is supposed to be.

3. Add the flour mixture to the creamed mixture alternately with the milk, beating after each addition, just until it is mixed.

4. Stir in the cranberries. (If you are using large commercial cranberries, chop them up a bit. Try a quick whir in the food processor.)

5. Spread the batter in a greased 9 x 13" (23 x 33 cm) pan. Bake in a 400°F (200°C) oven for 30–40 minutes, until golden brown and the top springs back when lightly touched.

CRANBERRY CAKE WITH BUTTER SAUCE (CONTINUED)

TO PREPARE THE BUTTER SAUCE

1. Combine the sauce ingredients in a saucepan and bring to a boil over medium heat, stirring constantly. Simmer for two minutes and remove from heat. A wire whisk is very useful to keep the sauce smooth.

NOTE

Serve the sauce warm over the cake - and remember - the secret is in the sauce. Be prepared for raves! (ummm! ahhh! ohhh!)

If you want to make this in a 9" (23 cm) square pan, just cut back on the ingredients by 1/3.

— desserts —

HELEN'S HEAVENLY CAKE

30 minutes

40 minutes

makes 1 cake

INGREDIENTS

3/4 cup	butter or margarine	175 mL
2 cups	sugar	500 mL
2	eggs	2
1 tsp.	vanilla	5 mL
2 1/2 cups	flour	625 mL
1/2 cup	cocoa	125 mL
2 tsp.	baking soda	10 mL
1/2 tsp.	salt	2 mL
2 cups	buttermilk or sour milk*	500 mL

Jeanne's quick Icing:

3 3/4 oz.	pkg. instant chocolate pudding	113 g
1 cup	whipping cream	250 mL

INSTRUCTIONS

1. To prepare the cake, in a large mixing bowl, cream together butter and sugar. Add eggs and vanilla and mix well.

2. In another bowl, mix flour, cocoa, baking soda and salt.

3. Add flour mixture to creamed mixture alternately with buttermilk, making three dry and two liquid additions, starting and ending with the flour. Mix just until blended.

4. Spread batter in well-greased baking pans, either 9 x 13" (23 x 33 cm) pan or two, 8" (20 cm) round pans if you are making a filling.

5. Bake in a 350°F (180°C) oven for 40 minutes, or until a toothpick inserted in the center comes out dry. Let the cake cool in the pan for five minutes before turning out on a rack to cool.

TO PREPARE JEANNE'S QUICK ICING

1. Prepare the pudding according to the package directions. Whip the cream until stiff.

2. Fold the whipped cream into the pudding mix and spread over the cooled cake.

NOTES

*For sour milk, add 2 tbsp. (30 mL) lemon juice or vinegar to 1 7/8 cups (460 mL) milk.

CINNAMON PECAN APPLE CAKE

30 minutes

1 hour

12-15 servings

INGREDIENTS

1 cup	vegetable oil	250 mL
2 cups	white sugar	500 mL
3	eggs	3
1 1/4 tsp.	vanilla	7 mL
2 cups	flour	500 mL
1 tsp.	salt	5 mL
1 tsp.	cinnamon	5 mL
1 tsp.	baking soda	5 mL
3 cups	pared, diced apples	750 mL
1 cup	chopped pecans or walnuts	250 mL

Caramel Topping:

1/2 cup	butter or margarine	125 mL
1 cup	brown sugar	250 mL
1/4 cup	milk	60 mL

INSTRUCTIONS

TO PREPARE THE CAKE

1. To make the cake, beat together oil, sugar, eggs and vanilla. Beat three minutes at medium speed if you are using a mixer, slightly longer if you are beating by hand.
2. Mix the flour, salt, cinnamon and baking soda and add to the sugar mixture. Mix well. Stir in the apples and nuts.
3. Spread the batter in a greased 9 x 13" (23 x 33 cm) pan and bake at 350°F (180°C) for 1 hour.

TO PREPARE THE CARAMEL TOPPING:

1. When the cake is almost finished baking, prepare the Caramel topping. In a heavy saucepan combine the topping ingredients and boil for 3 minutes.
2. Pour the caramel topping over the hot cake. Let the cake sit for a couple hours before serving.

COCONUT CREAM PIE

30 minutes

1/2 hour

15 servings

INGREDIENTS

Flaky Pastry:

1 3/4 cups	all-purpose flour	425 mL
3/4 tsp.	salt	3 mL
2/3 cup	lard (1/3 lb.)	150 mL
1	egg yolk	
1 1/2 tsp.	vinegar	7 mL
1/3 cup	cold water	75 mL

This recipe makes enough pastry for two crusts,
or one double crust pie.

Coconut Cream Filling:

1/4 cup	sugar	60 mL
3 tbsp.	cornstarch	45 mL
2 cups	milk	500 mL
2	eggs*, beaten	2
1 1/2 cups	coconut	375 mL
1 tsp.	vanilla	5 mL
1 cup	whipping cream, whipped	250 mL

INSTRUCTIONS

TO PREPARE CRUST

1. To make the pastry, mix the flour and salt and then cut in the lard with a pastry blender or two knives until the mixture resembles coarse crumbs.

2. Separate an egg yolk into a measuring cup. Add the vinegar and whisk with a fork. Fill to the 1/3 cup (75 mL) measure with cold water.

3. Add to the flour mixture and mix with a fork until it just clings together and cleans away from the side of the bowl.

4. Divide dough in half. Roll out pastry on a lightly floured surface and fold in half. Gently move the pastry to the pie plate and unfold. Coax the pastry into the plate and allow pastry to overhang edges to reduce shrinkage.

5. Bake pie shell in 350°F oven for 30 minutes or until browned.

TO PREPARE FILLING

1. Mix sugar and cornstarch in a saucepan. Gradually blend in the milk. Cook over medium heat, stirring constantly until mixture comes to a boil and thickens.

2. Add a little of the hot milk mixture to the beaten eggs, then return the eggs to the saucepan and stir well. Heat to boiling, stirring vigorously.

3. Remove cream filling from heat and add the coconut and vanilla. Allow to cool.

4. Fold in one cup (250 mL) whipped cream and pour it into the baked crust.

5. Top with remaining whipped cream. Chill and serve.

6. If desired, sprinkle with toasted coconut.

NOTE

*Since we are using whole eggs, the white may tend to cook in lumps. Just mix it with a hand blender until smooth. The flavor and texture will be lovely!

COCONUT CREME PIE

SUNSHINE BLUEBERRY MUFFINS

30 minutes

20 minutes

Makes 12 muffins

INGREDIENTS

1 3/4 cup	flour	425 mL
1/2 cup	sugar	125 mL
2 1/2 tsp.	baking powder	12 mL
3/4 tsp.	salt	3 mL
1	egg, well beaten	1
1/3 cup	vegetable oil	75 mL
3/4 cup	milk	175 mL
1 cup	blueberries (fresh or frozen)	250 mL
2 tbsp.	sugar	30 mL
2 tsp.	lemon rind, grated	10 mL

Lemon Sugar Topping:

2 tbsp.	butter, melted	30 mL
1/4 tsp.	lemon juice	1 mL
1/4 cup	sugar	60 mL

INSTRUCTIONS

1. In a large bowl, mix the flour with 1/2 cup (125 mL) sugar, baking powder and salt. Make a well in the center.

2. Combine the egg, oil and milk. Add to the dry ingredients, stirring until moistened.

3. Toss the blueberries with two tbsp. (30 mL) of sugar and the lemon rind. Fold into the batter. Fill a greased muffin pan or muffin cups 2/3 full and bake for 20 minutes at 400°F (200°C).

4. While the muffins bake, mix the butter and lemon juice. Remove the muffins from the pan and dip in the butter mixture and then into the remaining sugar. Place on a rack to cool.

SUNSHINE BLUEBERRY MUFFINS

breakfast
PHYLLO EGGS

20 minutes

15-20 minutes

6 Servings

INGREDIENTS

4 sheets	phyllo pastry	4
2 tbsp.	butter, melted	30 mL
4 tsp.	parmesan cheese, grated fresh	20 mL
6	eggs	6
2	green onions and/or fresh basil, finely chopped	2
	salt, pepper and cayenne to taste	
	butter for greasing tins	

INSTRUCTIONS

1. Brush sheet of phyllo with melted butter. Top with another sheet and brush with butter. Cut stack into six 4" (10 cm) squares. Repeat with remaining 2 sheets. Stack 3 squares together so corners do not overlap. Press into buttered muffin tins.

2. Sprinkle parmesan cheese into each phyllo-lined tin. Break 1 egg into each tin. Sprinkle with green onion and/or fresh basil, salt, pepper and cayenne.

3. Bake 15-20 minutes at 425°F (220°C). Pastry should be golden and eggs fully cooked.

NOTE

* This recipe is part of a new collection and does not appear in one of our published books. It has been adapted for use at our lodges from the Fabulous Fairholme cookbook

PHYLLO EGGS

BACON AND EGGS CASSEROLE

20 minutes

40-45 minutes

8-10 Servings

When serving a large group for breakfast, here is a simple way to present eggs. This is especially good for a buffet style brunch.

INGREDIENTS

4	bacon strips	4
18	eggs	18
1 cup	milk	250 mL
1 cup	shredded cheddar cheese	250 mL
1 cup	sour cream	250 mL
1/4 cup	sliced green onion	60 mL
1 tsp.	salt	5 mL
1/2 tsp.	pepper	2 mL

INSTRUCTIONS

1. Cook the bacon until crisp, then drain and crumble.
2. Beat the eggs and add the remaining ingredients to them. Pour egg mixture into a greased 9 x 13" (23 x 33 cm) casserole dish. Sprinkle the bacon on top.
3. Bake, UNCOVERED, at 325°F (160°C) for 40-45 minutes, or until set. Let sit 5 minutes before serving.

OVERNIGHT CHEESE STRADA

20 minutes

1 1/2 hours

12 Servings

INGREDIENTS

6 cups	bread cut in 1/2" (1.3 cm) cubes	1.5 L
2 cups	shredded medium or sharp cheddar cheese	500 mL
1 lb.	bacon, cooked and crumbled, or chopped ham	500g
1/4 cup	chopped green pepper	60 mL
6	large eggs	6
4 cups	whole milk	1 L
1 tsp.	dry mustard	5 mL
1/2 tsp.	salt	2 mL
1/4 tsp.	pepper	1 mL
1/4 cup	chopped green onion	60 mL
1/2 cup	butter or margarine, melted	125 mL

INSTRUCTIONS

1. Place half the bread cubes in the bottom of a greased 9 x 13" (23 x 33 cm) pan. Scatter the cheese, bacon and green pepper over the bread. Cover with the remainder of the bread cubes.

2. Beat the eggs with the milk, dry mustard, salt and pepper. Pour evenly over the bread cubes. Refrigerate overnight.

3. Before baking, sprinkle with green onions and drizzle with melted butter.

4. Set the pan in a pan of hot water. Bake uncovered at 300°F (150°C) for 1 1/2 hours.

SERVING SUGGESTION

We like to serve this with Blueberry or Cranberry Muffins, or warm Cinnamon Buns.

SOUR CREAM PANCAKES

15 minutes

15 minutes

makes 16 pancakes

This recipe has evolved at our house over the years and has spread far and wide. We have served these to people from all around the world and they always have seconds. They are great served with maple syrup or heaped with sweetened strawberries and piled high with whipped cream. Try adding fresh blueberries to the batter or serving them with Blueberry Sauce.

INGREDIENTS

2 cups	flour	500 mL
2 tsp.	baking powder	10 mL
1 tsp.	baking soda	5 mL
2 tsp.	sugar	10 mL
1/2 tsp.	salt	2 mL
2	eggs, slightly beaten	2
1/2 cup	sour cream	125 mL
2 cups	milk	500 mL

INSTRUCTIONS

1. In a large mixing bowl, mix together the flour, baking powder, baking soda, sugar and salt.

2. In a separate bowl, mix the eggs, sour cream and milk. Beat well with a wire whisk.

3. Pour the milk mixture into the dry ingredients and beat with the wire whisk until the batter is fairly smooth. A few small lumps won't hurt the pancakes.

4. Heat a greased griddle or heavy frying pan over medium-high heat. Pour batter onto the hot griddle and cook until the top is bubbly and the pancake is slightly dry around the edges. Turn and cook on the other side until golden brown.

NOTE

Now, I have to tell you that pancake preferences are kind of a personal thing. We like ours on the thinner, lighter side so I often add just a little more milk. With a little practice you can make them to your own liking.

APPLE PANCAKES

15 minutes   20-25 minutes   4 servings

A little bit of sweet for your breakfast, great for brunch, at home we even serve this for dinner when the "cook" gets lazy!

INGREDIENTS

3 tbsp.	butter or margarine	45 mL
4	apples, pared and sliced	4
1/4 cup	sugar, brown or white	60 mL
1 tsp.	cinnamon	5 mL
1 cup	milk	250 mL
6	eggs	6
1 cup	flour	250 mL
2 tsp.	white sugar	10 mL
1/2 tsp.	salt	2 mL

INSTRUCTIONS

1. In a 10" (25 cm), ovenproof pan, melt butter. Add apples, sugar and cinnamon and cook on the top of the stove until the apples are soft, about five minutes. Taste for sweetness.
2. Meanwhile, mix milk, eggs, flour, sugar and salt, beating well.
3. Pour the batter over the cooked apples. You may want to sprinkle some sugar and cinnamon over the batter for added flavor.
4. Bake, UNCOVERED, in a 425°F (220°C) oven for 20-25 minutes.

SERVING SUGGESTIONS

Cut the pancake in wedges and serve from the pan. Serve with maple syrup, sour cream or ice cream. This is also good on its own.

NOTE

For a thinner pancake, halve the ingredients for the batter but bake in the same-size pan. Reduce baking time by five minutes.

GINGER SNAPS

20 minutes

10 minutes

makes 2-3 dozen

If it's a crackle-topped gingersnap you crave, this one has always worked for us!

INGREDIENTS

3/4 cups	margarine or shortening	175 mL
1 cup	white sugar	250 mL
1	egg	1
1/4 cup	molasses	60 mL
2 cups	flour	500 mL
1 tsp.	baking soda	5 mL
1 tsp.	cinnamon	5 mL
1 tsp.	cloves	5 mL
1 tsp.	ginger	5 mL
	white sugar	

INSTRUCTIONS

1. Cream together margarine and sugar.
2. Beat in egg and molasses.
3. Mix flour, baking soda, cinnamon, cloves and ginger. Add to the creamed mixture.
4. Form heaping tablespoonfuls (15 mL plus) of dough into small balls, smaller than a golf ball.
5. Roll dough balls in sugar. Do not flatten.
6. Place balls 2" (5 cm) apart on an ungreased baking sheet and bake at 375°F (190°C) for 10 minutes, or until tops are crackled and lightly browned.
7. Let cookies cool 10 minutes on the baking sheet before removing them to a cooling rack.

NOTE

This recipe doubles well.

CARAMEL AGGRESSION COOKIES

20 minutes   12 minutes   makes 5 dozen

This firm, crunchy cookie with all its caramel goodness is too simple to ignore. It has been a long-time favourite of the Garry Webber family. He finally shared it with us – probably because the paper it was written on was almost worn out!

INGREDIENTS

3 cups	flour	750 mL
3 cups	brown sugar	750 mL
6 cups	rolled oats*	1.5 L
3 cups	butter	750 mL
1 tsp.	baking soda	5 mL
	sugar	

INSTRUCTIONS

1. Thoroughly knead together all the ingredients. Roll each cookie into a ball the size of a golf ball. Place each ball on an ungreased cookie sheet and flatten with your fingers or with the bottom of a glass dipped in sugar.

2. Bake at 350°F (180°C) for 12 minutes. Remove to a rack to cool.

NOTE

*Old-fashioned oats are recommended.

— cookies —

DOUBLE WHAMMY COOKIES

 20 minutes

 10-12 minutes

 makes 3-4 dozen

Are there many kids (big or little) who don't like chocolate and peanut butter? Better teach them how to make this recipe themselves, because they'll be begging you for more!

INGREDIENTS

1 cup	flour	250 mL
1/2 cup	cocoa	125 mL
2 tsp.	baking soda	10 mL
1 tsp.	baking powder	5 mL
3/4 cup	softened butter or margarine	175 mL
1/2 cup	peanut butter	125 mL
1 cup	white sugar	250 mL
2	eggs	2
1 cup	semisweet chocolate chips	250 mL
1 cup	peanut butter chips	250 mL

INSTRUCTIONS

1. In a small bowl, combine flour, cocoa, baking soda and baking powder.

2. In a large bowl, cream together the butter and peanut butter. Add sugar and eggs and beat well. Add the flour mixture and both kinds of chips. Stir until well combined.

3. Drop by teaspoonfuls (5 mL) on an ungreased cookie sheet. Do not press down. Bake at 350°F (180°C) for 10-12 minutes.

CPSIA information can be obtained
at www.ICGtesting.com
Printed in the USA
BVHW051640140621
609528BV00013B/2221

9 782252 382981